THE IDAHO COLLEGE MURDERS

Exposing the Shadows of Tragedy and Resilience in the Heartland of America.

Voice of The Victim

LEGAL NOTICE

DISCLAIMER

Every effort has made this book as complete and accurate as possible. This book provides information only up to the publishing date. Therefore, this book should be used as a guide, not the ultimate source.

The purpose of this book is to educate. The author and the publisher do not warrant that the information contained in this book is fully complete and shall not be responsible for any errors or omissions. The author and publisher shall have neither liability nor responsibility to any person or entity concerning any loss or damage caused or alleged to be caused directly or indirectly by this book.

Table Of Table

Introduction

There was a location where dreams grew root in the center of the charming town of Moscow, Idaho, where golden waves of grain met the blue skies. A place where young people sought information, formed friendships, and looked to the future with hope for a better day. It was a location where the hum of intellectual curiosity permeated the air and was enveloped in the soft embrace of academics.

But this ideal oasis of knowledge and optimism was plunged into darkness on a chilly November 2022 evening. In a rental property that was shared by four people, four lives that were full of potential and dreams were put to death only a short distance from the warm campus of the University of Idaho. Ethan Chapin, Kaylee Goncalves, Xana Kernodle, and Madison Mogen would have their futures snatched in an act of unimaginable brutality, and their names would be eternally inscribed into the history of this sleepy community.

This book, "The Idaho College Murders," takes readers on a trip through the gruesome mystery that engulfed Moscow, Idaho, as well as the hearts and minds of those who followed its horrific story. It is a tale of lost innocence, shattered lives, and the resiliency of a community in the face of unfathomable tragedy.

We will explore the murky alleyways of a crime that left law enforcement perplexed since it appeared to have no rhyme or purpose as we dive into the complexities of this case. We will investigate the mystery of Bryan Kohberger, a lone suspect whose intentions are yet unknown. The horrifying question of how he met the victims and the reason why their paths crossed in a terrible, fateful meeting will be one we mull about.

"The Idaho College Murders" is a monument to the resilience of the human spirit, despite its horrific aspects. It is a testament to the fortitude of a community that choose to come together in commemoration and healing rather than allow tragedy to define it. It serves as a reminder that despite terrible bloodshed, relationships of comradeship and hope may remain, illuminating the path to a better tomorrow.

We will try to find answers, closure, and justice as we unravel the threads of this chilling story in the pages that follow. We will honor those whose lives were cut short and the unwavering spirit of those who continue to honor their memory. The narrative of "The Idaho College Murders" serves as a reminder of the transience of life, the enduring strength of community, and the unflinching pursuit of the truth even in the most difficult circumstances. The trip you are about to go on will fascinate, astound, and ultimately inspire you.

Chapter 1

A Serene Campus Shattered

There are still oases of tranquility hidden throughout the enormous fabric of the American landscape, in spite of the fact that busy towns and gigantic metropolises dominate the horizon. These oases of tranquility appear to be unaffected by the inexorable march of time. One such haven of peace and quiet was the city of Moscow, Idaho, which was located in the center of the Pacific Northwest. It exemplified the very definition of rural quaintness with its undulating hills, lush farmlands, and breathtaking mountain ranges serving as a backdrop. However, hidden under its tranquil veneer was a bustling academic hub known as the University of Idaho, which was a place where the pursuit of both knowledge and dreams was an everyday occurrence.

The Peaceful Town of Moscow, Idaho

Moscow, which is frequently referred to as the "Heart of the Arts," had developed a reputation for being a refuge for creative types, intellectuals, and individuals who loved being outside. This reputation led to Moscow being dubbed the "Heart of the Arts." It was the type of town that smelled like freshly plowed soil blended with the aroma of freshly brewed coffee from the local coffee shops. The majority of the surrounding region was comprised of potato fields, and the residents took great pride in the close-knit community that they had developed. At this location, friendly smiles and polite greetings were as prevalent as the potatoes themselves.

The colorful history of the American West was inextricably intertwined with the history of the town. When Moscow was first established in the latter part of the 19th century, it functioned primarily as an agricultural community. Since that time, however, it has evolved into a bustling cultural and educational hub. Its streets were lined with historic buildings, each of which had a narrative to tell, and the people who lived there exemplified the spirit of the American frontier by being hardworking, resilient, and always prepared to explore new horizons.

The University of Idaho Community

The University of Idaho, which is located smack dab in the midst of this picture-perfect tiny town, is the institution that is responsible for the intellectual vitality of the community. In the year 1889, the institution was founded, and ever since that time, it has served as a symbol of the ever-present priority that the local community continues to place on education. This enormous institution was well recognized for its majestic redbrick buildings and well maintained grounds, so prospective students traveled from all across the United States to enroll in its programs. Thoughts were nurtured here, in the midst of the rustling leaves of towering trees; ideas were created here; and destiny were shaped here.

The University of Idaho was more than just a hub for higher education; it was also a tightly knit community, a place in which connections of friendship and camaraderie could be forged under the pressure cooker of academic research. The intellectual aspirations of the students were fed by their instructors, and the students, in turn, carried the torch of knowledge forward with ardor and enthusiasm. In other words, the school might be described as a melting pot due to the diverse range of cultures and academic fields that were represented there. The university served as a microcosm of the complex tapestry that formed the foundation of the nation.

The Fateful Day: November 13, 2022

On the other hand, on November 13, 2022, an incident that shattered the tranquility that had been the defining attribute of the town would take place, and it would leave an everlasting mark on the community that grew around the institution. When dawn dawned in Moscow, everyone was under the impression that it would be just another normal autumn day. However, what was to follow was a foreboding scene that no one could have possible predicted. It was a day that would not be able to be explained and would leave scars that time could only hope to heal, a day that would leave the town and the university with a day that would etch itself into the collective memory of the town and the institution. It was a day that would defy explanation and leave scars that time could only hope to heal.

At the same time as the sun was casting long shadows across the landscape, students ran around the campus with their heads held high and their back packs packed with textbooks and aspirations. In spite of the fact that winter was getting closer and there was a chill in the air, there was an unbreakable sense of safety that prevailed across the entire town. Nobody had any idea that by the end of the day, that feeling of safety would be irrevocably shattered, and it would be replaced with a profound and unsettling question: How could such a catastrophe occur in the heart of this peaceful campus? The government and the police were both completely clueless about what had taken place.

Chapter 2

The Victims

The world as a whole became aware, as a consequence of the Idaho College Murders, not only of the horrific act that had been committed, but also of the four young lives that had been tragically cut short as a result of the crime. In this chapter, we take a peek at the lives of the victims and the aspirations they had before their untimely deaths. Each of them was a unique and promising people whose untimely passing rocked the basis of their community.

Ethan Chapin, the Aspiring Engineer

At the time, Ethan Chapin was just 20 years old, but he had a dream that was as expansive as the boundless terrain of Idaho. It was obvious that he had a great interest in mechanics even at a young age, and he was well on his way to obtaining the position of engineer that he had always envisioned for himself. Even at a young age, it was evident that he had a strong interest in mechanics. Friends and family members remember his boundless curiosity and how they regularly came across him experimenting with a wide variety of tools and equipment in an effort to fathom the intricate workings of the complicated mechanics at work in the world around him.

Ethan already had a plan for his future that would lead to his success and happiness. At the University of Idaho, where he was pursuing a degree in engineering, he had won the sympathy and respect of his professors as a result of his exceptional success in his studies. His professors will always remember him as a responsible student, someone who was not only excited about the profession but also eager to aid his classmates in grasping the complexities of engineering. His students will always remember him as someone who was willing to help them understand the nuances of engineering. The National Society of Collegiate Scholars counted him as a member at one point. Ethan's ambitions didn't just entail accomplishing his own personal achievements; rather, he wanted to make the world a better place by being inventive and finding answers to issues. He accomplished this by focusing on the things that he could control, such as his own actions.

Kaylee Goncalves, the Vivacious Dancer

Kaylee Goncalves, who was 21 years old, with a vivacious attitude that was a perfect complement to the lively nature of her dance abilities. She was well-known in the dance community as "Kaylee Goncalves the Dancer." Her primary passion was dancing, and it was via this medium that she was able to express not only the most profound feelings that she had, but also the highest aspirations that she had for herself. Her loved ones have fond recollections of the contagious joy that she emanated both on and off the stage, and they attribute those memories to her.

They will have this recollection of her with them throughout their lives.

Kaylee, who has dance as her primary creative focus, demonstrated an exceptional level of attention to the area of dance while she was a student at the University of Idaho. Her performances were nothing short of extraordinary, and they left her audience enthralled and inspired. Her audience was left intrigued and driven by her performances. Her performances were nothing less than captivating to see in their entirety. She believed in the power of art to mend broken hearts and bring people together, and she dreamt of one day being able to teach and choreograph dances so that she could share her passion for dancing with the rest of the world. She felt that art had the capacity to heal broken hearts and bring people together.

Xana Kernodle, the Promising Artist

Xana Kernodle, who had just turned 20 years old at the time, demonstrated a level of skill that was much above average. Her skill as an artist was undeniable, and the body of work that she created exemplified the unmistakable worldview that she brought to everything she did. Whether it was via her paintings, sculptures, or even her digital art, Xana has an innate ability to create works of art that captured the essence of life's beauty and complexity.

During the time that Xana was attending the University of Idaho for her studies in the fine arts, her work was gaining a lot of attention both inside and outside of the academic community very quickly. Her creative creations weren't only a way for her to express herself; they were also meant to provoke contemplation and thought in the minds of those who had the opportunity to see them firsthand. The goal that Xana set for herself was to continue to break new ground in her field by employing her creative expression to challenge preconceived notions and inspire people to make constructive adjustments in their lives.

Madison Mogen, the Future Scientist

A young lady named Madison Mogen, who was 21 years old, had an insatiable need for learning that was beyond limits. She was working for a degree in science with the goal of having a career in which she might participate in the discovery of scientific findings that would have a significant impact on the future of the globe. Madison's passion for the natural world was contagious, and she had a profound dedication to the protection of the environment.

The commitment and intelligence that she showed in her studies at the University of Idaho astonished her teachers. The University of Madison was actively engaged in innovative research initiatives that investigated potential solutions to urgent environmental problems. She was adamant about being a part of the solution because she was under the impression that the scientific community had the answer to many of the most serious problems that humanity faced.

As we pay our respects to these extraordinary young people, it becomes abundantly evident that their ambitions were more than simply dreams; rather, they were guiding lights of hope and promise that were snuffed out much too soon. Their experiences serve as a powerful reminder of the enormous potential that lies within our young people, as well as the significance of valuing every life and every aspiration.

Chapter 3

A Murderous Mystery Unveiled

The evening of November 13th, 2022 had arrived in Moscow, Idaho, bringing with it a hauntingly quiet atmosphere. It was the type of peaceful evening that university towns are famous for, when the only sounds that could be heard were the rustling of leaves and the far-off murmuring of students. On the other hand, a menacing gloom was about to rise from behind this placid surface.

A Chilling Crime Scene

An urgent call to 911 disrupted the peace as the clock inched closer and closer to midnight. The caller's voice shook with fear as they related a horrible event that took place inside of a simple rental property that was located just a few blocks away from the campus of the University of Idaho. The rapidly flashing blue lights of the responding cops produced an unsettling glare on the otherwise peaceful streets as they arrived quickly.

As soon as they stepped inside the rented house, a terrifying scene greeted them.

Ethan Chapin, Kaylee Goncalves, Xana Kernodle, and Madison Mogen were the names of the young people whose lifeless bodies were found strewn over the floor of the living room. The walls gave testimony to a horrible conflict, as if the very chamber itself had absorbed the terror that had unfolded inside its limits. This was the case because the walls bore witness to the struggle.

The shocking level of violence displayed by the perpetrator of the act. Each person had been stabbed numerous times, and there was a distinct and heavy feeling of foreboding in the air. What in the world could have possessed someone to carry out such a horrific deed? Not only did the question trouble the investigators, but it also preoccupied the whole town.

The Initial Bafflement of Law Enforcement

After the first shock subsided and the grim reality of the situation sank in, the personnel in charge of law enforcement were faced with a difficult and perplexing dilemma. There was no indication that someone had attempted to break into the residence, and nothing out of the usual appeared to have transpired in the neighborhood. The town was rocked to its core by the shocking news of the triple homicide, which was an event of such magnitude that it had never happened before. Because there was a low percentage of violent crime in the city, incidents like this one were extremely uncommon.

At the scene of the event, a significant number of law enforcement personnel descended, including investigators and officers from the Moscow Police Department, the Latah County Sheriff's Office, and the University of Idaho Campus Security. The first item on their list was to secure the location and guarantee the residents of the neighboring communities that they were in a secure environment. After that, they commenced the tedious process of documenting the crime scene, gathering evidence, and questioning potential witnesses.

It was clear that individuals in charge of enforcing the regulation first struggled with feeling confused about their responsibilities. They were at a loss for answers because this was not a typical crime scene, and there were no obvious clues as to why the crime had been committed, thus there was no way for them to determine why the crime had been committed. It is even more challenging to fathom the terrible event that took place in Moscow, Idaho given that the city has a history of having a reputation for having a low crime rate and a culture that is serene.

The Hunt for Clues Begins

In the morning, as soon as the first rays of sunshine emerged, people immediately began looking for clues and information in earnest. A comprehensive investigation of the crime site was carried out by forensic experts, who were looking for any crumb of evidence that would shed light on the identity of the perpetrator or the reasons behind the act. When collecting and analyzing fingerprints, blood spatter patterns, and DNA samples, a considerable deal of caution and attention to specifics was used throughout the process.

Simultaneously, investigators started making contact with the victims' acquaintances, family members, and other persons who knew them well in order to recreate the victims' final moments of life. The purpose of this was to determine what happened in their final moments of life. What were they engaged in throughout the hours and minutes leading up to the catastrophic event? Who among those had been their primary point of communication? Have any of them expressed worries or suspicions about another individual or made statements to that effect?

The area was gripped with fear and worry, and as a direct response, community members joined together to offer support and assistance to one another. People began to contribute whatever information they had that they considered would be useful to the investigation in the form of anonymous tips that began to trickle in as vigils were arranged as a way to remember those who had passed away and to pay respect to those who had been killed.

In Chapter 3, we explore into the early stages of the investigation, during which law enforcement officials are forced to confront the chilling crime scene, struggle with the inexplicable nature of the crime, and embark on the relentless hunt for clues that would ultimately lead them to the shocking revelation of a suspect in "The Idaho College Murders."

Chapter 4

The Arrest of Bryan Kohberger

After the horrific killings that rocked the people of Moscow, Idaho, as well as the campus of the University of Idaho, a feeling of dread and panic penetrated the chilly winter air like a heavy blanket following the events. Both the authorities who were investigating the killings that took place at the Idaho College and the general public were left with more questions than answers as a result of the mystery that surrounded the deaths that took place at the Idaho College. Nevertheless, as the hours turned into days, the relentless quest of justice would finally result in a breakthrough that would cause a change in the direction that this tragic tragedy would follow.

The 28-year-old Criminology Ph.D. Student

As the investigation into the killings advanced, law enforcement officers discovered that they were hunting for a suspect who was completely unexpected. Bryan Kohberger, a criminology Ph.D. student at Washington State University, was the 28-year-old suspect in this case. The past of Kohberger, which includes his participation in the research of criminal behavior, cast a suspicious pall over the probe.

To those who were familiar with Bryan Kohberger, he had always conveyed the image of being the archetypal graduate student, although one with a concerning fixation with the criminal underground and illicit behavior. His need to learn had taken him to the halls of academia, where he dived deeply into the complexity of aberrant behavior in humans. His quest for information had brought him there. He gave off the appearance to those who were close to him that he was an intellectual observer; he never prompted anybody to raise an eyebrow, and he was most certainly not a primary suspect in a terrible quadruple homicide.

Despite this, when the investigators dug more into his history, a picture that was more complicated and frightening began to emerge. A mind capable of unspeakable savagery existed underneath the outer manner of the humble student, and it was quickly revealed that this fact would soon send shockwaves across the academic world and beyond. The activities of the student would shortly cause shockwaves to be felt all across the world.

The Breakthrough in Pennsylvania

The inquiry into Bryan Kohberger's location directed detectives to go on a laborious and extensive search for him across many states. The search was expanded to include neighboring states as well. Pennsylvania, a very far distance from the tranquil streets of Moscow, was the location where the breakthrough that was absolutely essential took place. On December 30, 2022, law enforcement officials were successful in capturing Kohberger, and he was subsequently placed in custody at that time.

The actual arrest was a tense and exciting turning point in the unfolding narrative of the killings that took place at Idaho College. It was the end of a manhunt that had caught the interest of the entire country, but it also generated a lot of questions about Kohberger's route and his link to the victims.

The Long Road to Justice

The process of bringing those guilty to justice could finally be started once the person responsible for the crime, Bryan Kohberger, was arrested and placed under custody. The trip that was still in front of them was guaranteed to be an arduous one that would last for a very long time and be fraught with challenges at every turn. People who attended the University of Idaho and those who lived in the surrounding town of Moscow were in an extreme need for information. Not only did they want to understand why such a senseless act of violence had taken place, but they also wanted to make sure that those responsible were held accountable for their crimes.

While Kohberger awaited his trial in the confines of the Latah County Jail in Moscow, Idaho, the court system was gearing up to ensure a thorough and impartial review of the case. This was done while Kohberger was in custody. As a result of the Idaho College Murders, the community had been left with an indelible scar, and this wound needed to be healed before the community can go on.

In Chapter 4, we go into the horrifying shift that Bryan Kohberger went through from being a criminology student to a probable suspect in a murder case. Kohberger moved from being a student of criminology to a possible suspect in a murder case. We explore the dramatic events that led to his capture in Pennsylvania, and we will begin to study the long and winding journey toward justice, which would be characterized by the quest for truth and closure in the days that were to follow.

Chapter 5

The Motive Unknown

In the wake of the Idaho College Murders, one haunting question loomed large over the heads of those responsible for the investigation, the families of the victims, and the society at large; that question was why? Why would someone commit such a horrible crime, taking the lives of four young individuals who had their whole life in front of them, and why would they do it in such a heartless way? The fifth chapter of "The Idaho College Murders" delves further into the enigma of the reason, or more particularly, the lack of a purpose, for the killings that took place.

A Crime Without a Clear Reason

One of the aspects that produced the most bewilderment and left the most questions unanswered was the seeming absence of a clear reason for this calamity. This was one of the qualities that left the most questions unanswered. Motives like as envy, vengeance, financial gain, or any other form of personal animosity can frequently be found in homicide investigations. The victim was killed as a result of these circumstances in a significant number of these cases. However, despite the detectives' meticulous study of the evidence, as well as their interviews with witnesses and investigation into the pasts of both the victims and the suspect, they were unable to find any credible explanation for the crime. This was the case despite the fact that they interviewed witnesses and conducted research into the histories of both the victims and the suspect. There was no evidence to show that Bryan Kohberger had any ties to any of the victims, which would have constituted a convincing explanation for their homicides if such associations existed. If the evidence had been different, we might have been able to conclude that Bryan Kohberger was responsible for their deaths.

The fact that there was no credible explanation for what had taken place made a situation that was already perplexing far more so. It left law enforcement with the arduous responsibility of not just obtaining evidence but also attempting to comprehend the psychological make-up of the individual who committed the crime, which is a tremendous obstacle to overcome. Because there was no clear motive for the offense, it was as if they were attempting to navigate a labyrinth without a guide. This made the investigation much more difficult. In order to uncover the truth, they had no choice but to rely on forensic science, behavioral analysis, and pure perseverance.

Unraveling the Mind of a Killer

Attempting to put oneself in the mindset of a killer is a task that is fraught with difficulty and difficulty. What possible reasons may there be for a person to carry out an act that is both nonsensical and violent at the same time? The psychological complications that come into play while attempting to comprehend the actions of a person like Bryan Kohberger are discussed in Chapter 5. We delve into the subjects of criminology and forensic psychology, shedding light on the methods and techniques that are used by experts in order to profile criminals and understand the thinking processes that are behind their acts.

Attempts by forensic psychiatrists, criminal profilers, and detectives to piece together the jigsaw puzzle that was Kohberger's mind took a significant amount of time and effort. They studied his history, looking at his behavior in the past as well as any possible symptoms of psychopathy or other mental health difficulties that may give insight into his reasons for acting in the manner that he did. In other words, they tried to figure out why he behaved in the manner that he did. The objective was very clear: to construct a profile of the killer in the hopes of shedding some light on the opaque reason for the killings. This was the aim.

As we begin to explore the realm of forensic psychology, some of the topics that we will look at include the complexities of criminal behavior, the factors that might influence an individual's decision to travel down a dangerous path, and the challenges that come with seeing warning signs before a disaster takes place. It gives the reader a glimpse into the minds of those people who have spent their entire lives to the pursuit of justice and a knowledge of the darker parts of human behavior.

Questions That Linger

As a consequence of the unfathomable brutality of the killings and the incomprehensible impulses that led to them, the Idaho College Murders pose questions to which we may never have acceptable replies. This is because of the incomprehensible motivations that led to the atrocities. The following are some of the questions that come to mind after reading Chapter 5: To what degree do you think it's possible for us to ever aspire to understand how the mind of a serial murderer works? Is it still possible to come to grips with something that occurred when the reason why it occurred cannot be determined? What does the fact that there is no apparent motivation tell us about the nature of violence itself, specifically?

Within the context of "The Idaho College Murders," the pursuit of justice is closely linked to the inquiry of what took place. This chapter questions our views about the motivations behind acts of violence and exposes the sad truth that certain issues may remain unresolved, permanently casting a shadow over even the most thoroughly investigated crimes. In addition, this chapter calls attention to the fact that certain situations may remain unanswered. In Chapter 5, the author challenges the reader's preconceived notions about the reasons that people commit acts of violence by having them grapple with the puzzle of purpose.

Chapter 6

Connection or Coincidence?

After the tragic killings that sent shockwaves through the community of the University of Idaho and the city of Moscow, Idaho, there was one question that loomed large and remained unanswered in the aftermath of the events: What part did Bryan Kohberger have in the deaths of Ethan Chapin, Kaylee Goncalves, Xana Kernodle, and Madison Mogen, who were all thought to have been killed by him? Kohberger is in the process of earning his doctorate in criminology and is 28 years old. What drew them together on that fateful night in November? Was it some sort of sinister plan, or was it simply a curious coincidence?

As the investigators pored over the many pieces of evidence, they came upon a convoluted maze of linkages, both overt and covert, that seemed to defy easy explanation. Bryan Kohberger, a person whose academic interests should have kept him far away from the mayhem of a crime scene, emerged as a major player in this baffling story. The story is a bit of a mystery. Kohberger's scholarly pursuits ought to have kept him at a safe distance from the chaos of the crime scene.

As the investigators dug deeper into Kohberger's past, the mysteries surrounding his relationships to the victims began to reveal themselves. His public profile was that of an unassuming doctoral student who was immersing himself in the nuances of criminology, psychology, and law enforcement. However, he was actually a criminal mastermind. On the other hand, concealed under this apparent air of serenity was a network of associations that raised more questions than it provided answers.

Were there any extracurricular classes or activities that Kohberger engaged in with the victims that brought him into contact with them? They must have passed each other in the congested streets of Moscow; was it just coincidence that brought them together? Or, was there a more sinister relationship that was concealed from the curious eyes of law enforcement officials because it was kept at a higher level?

throughout order to find answers to the questions that they had, the detectives started their investigation by delving into the complex web of ties that had developed around the lives of both the victims and the suspect throughout the course of their investigation. The detectives looked at everyone from close friends and family members to casual acquaintances and even brief meetings in their search for the elusive linkages that connected the numerous lives that were the subject of the study.

It was one of those paradoxical realities where an apparently little detail, a chance touch, or a mutual passion may unwittingly generate relationships between folks who otherwise may not have ever crossed paths with one another. As the terrible truth started to come to light, it was clear that this was one of those contradictory realities. It was a depiction of a town that had been profoundly changed by the unfathomable violence that had befallen it, and it was shown as a tapestry of human ties that were both delicate and robust. This was a picture of a community that had been profoundly affected by the unfathomable atrocity that had befallen it.

As we move forward through the pages of this chapter, we will delve further into the complexity of these linkages in an effort to shed some light on the significant issues that troubled both the city of Moscow and the University of Idaho. These issues were a concern for both of these institutions. What can we infer from these connections concerning the suspect's mental condition as well as the lives of the persons who were wrongfully accused? Were they truly just a series of coincidences, or did they provide a glimpse into the heart of a mystery that had caused havoc on the social fabric of a town that had been relatively peaceful?

These answers may be discovered in traces of history, both personal histories and common histories, which contain the keys to solving the mystery of "The Idaho College Murders." As we are about to find out, the solutions may not only be found in the present, but also in the past; these answers may be found in traces of history, both personal histories and communal histories. In the shadows of this horrific tragedy, the intricacies of human connections, both known and hidden, emerge to the foreground, asking us to uncover the truth that lies beneath the surface of a murder that defies easy explanation. [Calls us] to find the truth that lies beneath the surface of a murder that defies easy explanation.

Chapter 8

Healing a Broken Community

As a result of the killings that took place at Idaho College, the city of Moscow, Idaho, was engulfed in a web of grief, fear, and bewilderment after the events. The formerly peaceful community was left with a wound that was difficult to heal and a scar that ran deep throughout the town after the event. As a direct result of the passing of Ethan Chapin, Kaylee Goncalves, Xana Kernodle, and Madison Mogen, shockwaves were felt across the community of the University of Idaho and beyond. Nevertheless, in spite of this unimaginable disaster, the human spirit has shown to be extremely resilient.

The Scars That Remain

As a consequence of the tragic events that took place in Moscow on November 13, 2022, every single person who named the city their home was left with not only physical but also emotional scars. Everyone was left with a profound impression as a result of the senselessness of the crime, and it served as a sobering reminder that one's goal of protection and security may be undermined in a single instant. The new normal for many individuals who were a part of this tight-knit society included sleepless nights, cheeks that were stained with tears, and an overarching sensation that they were vulnerable as a collective.

Each individual who had been adversely affected by the loss went through a grieving process that was entirely unique to them. Some people sought solace by retreating inside and attempting to grapple on their own, in solitude, with the pain that they were experiencing. Others found comfort in the loving embrace of their friends and family members, who reminisced about happier times in order to keep the memories alive. This helped them to cope with the difficult situation. On the other hand, the road to recovery was a difficult and difficult one, fraught with grief and unresolved worries for all those who were involved.

University Support and Counseling

After suffering such a devastating loss, the University of Idaho wasted no time in mobilizing its professors and staff members to get the assistance they needed as soon as it was humanly feasible. People who were having trouble dealing with the emotional aftermath of the killings were able to take use of a safe space that was made accessible by the counseling services at the university, which expanded its outreach after realizing there was a need for expert guidance.

Counselors with years of experience and training in the treatment of trauma and loss were on hand to lend an understanding ear and a calming presence to anyone required them. The participation in group therapy sessions resulted in the development of a sense of camaraderie and understanding, both of which were necessary components of the healing process. These sessions were especially tailored to meet the distinctive requirements of each person who had been affected by the event.

The population that resided within the facility gradually came to the conclusion that the road to healing was not a direct one. It was a twisting journey that was dotted with both setbacks and fleeting flashes of promise at various points along the way. On the other hand, the depth of the relationships inside the community increased with every single session of treatment, every single conversation that was had in common, and every single development that was made. Moscow, Idaho was not the only place in the state to suffer, and the community came together under the common goal of thriving in spite of the hardships.

The Moscow Community Coming Together

After suffering such a devastating loss, the University of Idaho wasted no time in mobilizing its professors and staff members to get the assistance they needed as soon as it was humanly feasible. People who were having trouble dealing with the emotional aftermath of the killings were able to take use of a safe space that was made accessible by the counseling services at the university, which expanded its outreach after realizing there was a need for expert guidance.

Counselors with years of experience and training in the treatment of trauma and loss were on hand to lend an understanding ear and a calming presence to anyone required them. The participation in group therapy sessions resulted in the development of a sense of camaraderie and understanding, both of which were necessary components of the healing process. These sessions were especially tailored to meet the distinctive requirements of each person who had been affected by the event.

The population that resided within the facility gradually came to the conclusion that the road to healing was not a direct one. It was a twisting journey that was dotted with both setbacks and fleeting flashes of promise at various points along the way. On the other hand, the depth of the relationships inside the community increased with every single session of treatment, every single conversation that was had in common, and every single development that was made. Moscow, Idaho was not the only place in the state to suffer, and the community came together under the common goal of thriving in spite of the hardships.

Chapter 9

Remembering the Lost

In the calm moments of contemplation, as the dark shadows of sadness crept over Moscow, a community realized that it was tied together by a single thread: a profound feeling of loss and an unwavering commitment to remember and celebrate four lives that were ruthlessly cut short. This realization occurred as the city was enveloped in the gloomy shadows of mourning. This was the common ground on which the community could come together. Chapter 9 of "The Idaho College Murders" is a testament to the lasting power of remembering as well as the persistent spirit of a community determined to find meaning in sorrow. This chapter represents the culmination of the investigation into the murders that took place at Idaho College. This section was taken from the book titled "The Idaho College Murders."

Paying Tribute to Ethan Chapin:

Ethan Chapin was known not just for his academic prowess but also for his contagious joy for life. He was an ambitious engineer who had a passion for creation, and he was driven to create new things. Friends and family members created a picture of a young man who had an exceptional potential to turn challenges into opportunities. This young man was always ready with a smile, believed in the power of education, and had a remarkable capacity to change things for the better. The farther we dive into Ethan's background, the more we find out about the goals he treasured and the legacies he left behind. This provides the readers with a glimpse into a life that was cut short due to a tragic occurrence, and it is a bittersweet experience for everybody involved.

Celebrating the Spirit of Kaylee Goncalves:

Kaylee Goncalves, a vibrant dancer who was full of energy, stood out as a bright example of innovation and vibrancy in the room. Her enthusiasm for dance had no bounds, and the level of dedication with which she approached the art form served as a model for those who were fortunate enough to be in her life. This chapter chronicles Kaylee's journey from the time she was a student in the dance department at the University of Idaho to the stages she graced, where she left an indelible impression on the hearts of all those who witnessed her perform. This chapter begins with Kaylee as a freshman in the dance department at the University of Idaho. It is a celebration of a life that was dedicated to art as well as a tribute to the way in which her passion continues to inspire other people. The life that was dedicated to art is being honored by this monument.

Xana Kernodle: A Legacy of Artistry:

Xana Kernodle's life was a canvas, and the art that she created was the language that she used to express herself. In this section, we look at the tremendous impact that Xana's creative output had on the individuals who were living in Moscow at the time. Those who investigated her artwork discovered that it provided them with the opportunity to convey their ideas and emotions via the utilization of visually stunning images and subject matter that stimulated contemplation. As we read through her writings, we muse about the concepts that she intended to convey to her audience and the discussions that she sparked. The story of Xana is not just a sad one; rather, it is a story about how the enduring power of art can touch the most fundamental aspects of who we are as individuals.

Madison Mogen: A Future Scientist's Legacy

Madison Mogen, a young woman with aspirations in the scientific field, often daydreamed about the possibility of one day inhabiting a universe in which new information and concepts were unearthed on a regular basis. Her unrelenting commitment to both her scholastic endeavors and her ambition to have a positive effect on the world was something that everyone who knew her could attest to. In this chapter, we look into Madison's academic interests, her goals, and the method in which she sought to bridge the gap between science and humanity in her quest to bridge the gap between science and humanity. In this chapter, we look into Madison's academic interests, her goals, and the manner in which she sought to bridge the gap between science and humanity. We are in the fortunate position of being able to watch how her legacy continues to inspire a new generation of scientists who are eager to follow in her footsteps.

Finding Strength Through Unity

As we pay our respects to these four remarkable individuals, we are reminded of how a community came together to heal and to commemorate what had transpired. Through the conducting of candlelight vigils, memorial services, and acts of goodwill for strangers, the city of Moscow, Idaho, displayed the power of community in the face of adversity by demonstrating the resilience of togetherness. This section takes a look at the strength of a community as it rallied around the families of the victims, offering support, consolation, and a shared desire to ensure that the memories of Ethan, Kaylee, Xana, and Madison be preserved for generations to come.

The ninth chapter of "The Idaho College Murders" isn't just a reminder of the lives that were cut short; rather, it's a celebration of the lives that were truly lived before they were snatched away. It is a powerful reminder that the human spirit can shine brilliantly even in the most difficult of situations, drawing strength from unity, and leaving a legacy that is greater than sadness. This serves as a poignant reminder that the human spirit can shine brilliantly even in the most trying of circumstances.

Chapter 10

Lessons from Tragedy

A glimmer of light arose in the aftermath of the unfathomable darkness that poured over Moscow, Idaho, on that dreadful night in November, serving as a monument to the tenacious human spirit and the resiliency of a city united in mourning. The tenth chapter of "The Idaho College Murders" looks into the deep lessons that may be drawn from the worst of tragedies. These are teachings that go beyond the borders of a single community and extend into the very essence of our common humanity.

The Senselessness of Violence

The first thing that we need to understand, which is something that eats away at the very heart of our collective awareness, is that violence serves no purpose. This is something that we need to learn because it is something that eats away at us. When we are compelled to confront the harrowing reality of lives that have been cut short in a manner that is incomprehensible, we are compelled to engage in a struggle with the age-old issue of why. What could possible motivate someone to do such awful atrocities, especially those committed against innocent people? This question worried community people and those who worked on the case during the inquiry into the homicides that took place at the Idaho College; it loomed like a sinister specter over the probe.

As we explore deeper into this troublesome aspect of the human condition, we are compelled to face the unsettling reality that the reasons behind acts of violence are not always evident. This is a reality that we are forced to face because it is a reality that we are compelled to face because it is a reality. It serves as a jarring reminder that even in the midst of the calmest and most perfect situations in our lives, darkness may emerge, compelling us to do battle with the unfathomable.

The purpose of this chapter is to conduct interviews with professionals in the domains of criminology, psychology, and sociology in order to gain a comprehensive understanding of the thought processes of those who study violent behavior. The purpose of these interviews is to shed insight on the complex network of factors that may have led to such disastrous outcomes. We are compelled to face the dreadful reality that, at times, it is possible that there are no straightforward solutions; instead, there is a horrifying void where knowledge ought to be located.

The Resilience of a Community

Despite this, the gloom of despondency illuminates a second, more upbeat lesson: the persistence with which a society may recover from disaster. Moscow, Idaho is a community that may be irreparably changed as a result of the Idaho College killings; yet, it is also a town that has firmly refused to be defined by those killings. The community may be permanently changed, but Moscow, Idaho is a town that has steadfastly refused to be defined by those murders. In the face of a catastrophe that could not even be imagined, the residents of the town rallied together to demonstrate to the rest of the world that their cohesion was the source of their resilience.

This chapter paints a clear picture of the strong sense of community that existed across the whole town. It tells the stories of neighbors comforting one another, of the University of Idaho offering steadfast support to its students and workers, and of the numerous acts of charity and compassion that blazed the route towards healing for those who were impacted by the disaster.

By conducting interviews with survivors, members of their families, and leaders of the community, we are able to get insight into the unbreakable bonds that were forged in the crucible of their suffering. We study the numerous ways in which individuals and groups worked together to pay respect to the memory of the victims, making ensuring that their legacy would not simply be one of sadness but also of togetherness and hope in the face of hardship.

The Enduring Legacy of The Idaho College Murders

The final half of this chapter dives into the impact that the Idaho College Murders have left behind, a legacy that is felt well beyond the limits of the city of Moscow. The memories of Ethan Chapin, Kaylee Goncalves, Xana Kernodle, and Madison Mogen serve as a potent reminder of the precious nature of life and the necessity of keeping vigilant in the battle against acts of violence. This is especially important in light of the recent school shooting in Florida that claimed the lives of 17 people.

Their experiences have prompted new initiatives on college campuses all around the country, with the aims of preventing tragedies of a similar type and building a culture of safety and support for students. These new efforts are aimed at preventing tragedies of a similar character as well as preventing tragedies of a similar kind. We study the many different ways in which advocacy organizations, academic institutions, and government agencies have worked together in order to honor the victims by striving towards a safer and more compassionate future.

The book "The Idaho College Murders" urges readers to reflect on these lessons, to come to grips with the unsettling reality of violence, and to draw encouragement from the tenacity of a community that refused to be ripped apart by the events that unfolded. The murders at the Idaho college took place in the early 1990s. This is a chapter that praises the enduring power of cooperation, compassion, and the unrelenting drive for a better tomorrow, while at the same time encouraging us to confront the darker side of human nature.

Conclusion

As we come to the end of our trip through the awful events that transpired in Moscow, Idaho, on that dreadful night in November, we are left with a profound sense of both sorrow and resilience. This comes as we approach the finish of our journey through the catastrophic events that transpired. "The Idaho College Murders" has led us through the darkest recesses of human life, where lives were cruelly cut short, hopes were destroyed, and a once-peaceful town was left reeling in shock.

The brutal slayings of Ethan Chapin, Kaylee Goncalves, Xana Kernodle, and Madison Mogen serve as a harrowing illustration of the fact that evil can infiltrate even the calmest of environments. It pushes us to confront the disturbing reality that violence may strike anyone, anytime, and it poses a challenge to our preconceived conceptions of safety. The questions that have persisted throughout this tale, such as the motivation, the link, and the why, continue to stay eerily unsolved, which is a monument to the ever-present mysteries of the human psyche.

In spite of the darkness and the many issues that remain unsolved, there are still glimmers of optimism and significant life lessons that may be gleaned from this tragedy. The tenacious spirit of mankind is on display in the way that both the

Moscow community and the University of Idaho have bounced back from recent tragedies. In the face of an unfathomable tragedy, they banded together in order to provide one another with support, compassion, and fortitude.

"The Idaho College Murders" has showed us that even in the aftermath of horrific violence, we still have the ability to choose how we react to it. This is something that is empowering. The legacy of the four young lives that were cut short that night is not determined by the senselessness of their deaths, but rather by the influence they had on the people who knew them and on the community at large. Their names will not be remembered as those of victims, but rather as reminders of the splendor of human potential, the importance of valuing education, and the necessity of savoring the time we spend with those we care about.

We are reminded of the resiliency of the human spirit, the relationships that bind us together in times of suffering, and the power that we find in pursuing justice as we reflect on this tale. The murders that took place at the Idaho State University may continue to be a mystery in many respects, but they have also served as a driving force for positive social transformation by encouraging communities to reassess their approaches to public safety and the significance of offering assistance to people whose lives have been upended by acts of violence.

In conclusion, we need to make sure that the lessons we've learned from the darkness aren't lost. We must not just remember Ethan, Kaylee, Xana, and Madison as victims, but also as models for a future in which there is no place for senseless murder. Let our remembrance of them serve as a rallying cry, a gentle nudge to keep the ties of community strong, and an illustration of our community's capacity to unearth rays of hope even in the most trying of circumstances.

The book "The Idaho College Murders" is more than just a recounting of a terrible event; rather, it is a testimony to the resiliency of the human spirit and the never-ending search for justice and healing. We pray that it will be a fitting memorial to those we have lost and a source of motivation for a better, more compassionate, and more secure future.

THE END

Made in the USA
Columbia, SC
09 August 2024

40117180R00052